Mystic Mandalas

Pure Prosperity

ATTRACTING ABUNDANCE

With Colour

Patricia Sereno

IMAGO MYSTIC ARTS / CANADA

IMAGO
MYSTIC ARTS

IMAGO MYSTIC ARTS
201A 4th St NE, Suite #402
Calgary, AB T2E 3S1

This book is not intended as a substitute for the medical advice of physicians. The reader should regularly consult a physician in matters relating to his/her health and particularly with respect to any symptoms that may require diagnosis or medical attention.

FIRST EDITION IMAGO MYSTIC ARTS NOVEMBER 2016
SECOND EDITION IMAGO MYSTIC ARTS MAY 2021
THIRD EDITION IMAGO MYSTIC ARTS FEBRUARY 2024

IMAGOMYSTICARTS.COM

ISBN: 978-1-988623-05-4 (Paperback)

PRINTED IN THE UNITED STATES OF AMERICA

Pure Prosperity

Belongs to :

_____

No Boundaries

Creation holds no limits

No boundaries apply

There is no quota on abundance

When the boundary is the sky

Nothing is withheld from me

I am offered every source

To claim the destiny I dream of

I need only chart my course

~Elizabeth D. Gray~

Pure Prosperity

Pure Prosperity

The Pure Prosperity Colouring Journal is a uniquely designed tool that allows you to explore your creativity and unleash your innate potential to attract abundance into your life. We commonly focus on our limitations and what we lack in life, which can make it challenging to imagine having more or better things. However, Pure Prosperity is about living without lack or scarcity; abundance is the natural state of the world and our being.

This Pure Prosperity Colouring Journal encourages you to focus on the abundance and prosperity surrounding you. As you colour, you can tap into your unconscious mind and discover your heart's desires. You will be able to identify areas where you seek improvement, whether it's financial wealth, career growth, healthy relationships, or personal achievements.

The abundance of nature inspires us to attract pure prosperity into our lives. Nature is abundant, from the countless leaves on a tree to the numerous petals on a flower. Similarly, when nurtured, the seeds of potential within us can create Pure Prosperity.

You will feel empowered and inspired as you colour your way through the Pure Prosperity Colouring Journal. You can focus on what you want to attract in your life and manifest it into reality. You will be amazed at how quickly your unconscious mind brings your deepest desires to the surface of your conscious mind and how easily you can attract abundance into your life.

This Pure Prosperity Colouring Journal is a powerful tool for attracting abundance, prosperity, and success into your life. With its help, you can unleash your creativity and tap into your inherent potential to create a life of pure prosperity and abundance.

Mystic Mandalas

A Journey into the Heart of Mystic Mandalas

Welcome to a journey into the world of Mystic Mandalas. This adult colouring journal is not just a collection of designs; it's a gateway to a world of peace, self-expression, and inner discovery. Here, you will find more than just pages to colour; you will embark on a creative voyage that intertwines art, spirituality, and mindfulness. As you delve into each mandala, you're stepping into a sacred space where colours and shapes transcend mere visuals and become a medium for personal growth, food for the soul and tranquillity for your mind.

Mandalas are Symbols of Unity and Continuity

The concept of a mandala, which means "sacred circle" in Sanskrit, embodies the ideas of wholeness, unity, and the infinite nature of life. Mandalas have a rich history and are revered in various cultures worldwide. You'll find them in the spiritual symbols of First Nations medicine wheels, in the serene Zen circle paintings, and intricately woven into the architecture and stained glass of mosques, temples, and cathedrals. These designs aren't just artistic; they're deeply symbolic.

Nature and Mandalas: A Reflection of the Cosmos

Mandalas are a natural part of the world. They mirror the circular shapes of our planet, the Sun, the Moon, and other celestial bodies. But they're more than just shapes. Mandalas represent the circles of our lives, the ever-turning wheels of relationships that include our partners, families, friends, and broader communities.

The Healing Power of Colouring Mandalas

Colouring these Mystic Mandalas offers a serene escape from the hustle and bustle of everyday life. It's a therapeutic activity that can help soothe your mind, reduce stress, and alleviate anxiety. As you fill these sacred circles with colour, you're not just creating art but engaging in meditation. This meditative colouring can help you release mental and emotional blockages, let go of the old, and welcome new insights and possibilities into your life.

Your Personal Journey of Mindfulness and Creativity

As you pick up your colouring tools and start this journey, you do more than just colouring within the lines. You're connecting with a tradition that spans cultures and centuries. Each stroke and choice of colour is a step towards understanding yourself better. It's an opportunity to reflect, relax, and even find solutions to the challenges you face in daily life.

An Invitation to Explore and Grow

We invite you to take this time for yourself. Sit comfortably, and let the colours and patterns flow onto the page from your heart and soul. As you progress through each mandala, observe the feelings and thoughts that arise. Embrace this process as a form of creative therapy, a way to connect with the deeper parts of yourself.

In colouring these Mystic Mandalas, you're not just engaging in a hobby; you're participating in a practice of mindfulness and self-discovery. Allow yourself to be immersed in the moment's beauty, finding peace and joy in the simple act of colouring. Welcome to the transformative experience of Mystic Mandalas.

The Transformative Power of Mystic Mandalas

In your journey with Mystic Mandalas, remember that each page you've coloured is a testament to your journey within. This experience is more than just an artistic endeavour; it is a voyage of your heart and mind, an exploration of your inner world through the meditative art of colouring.

The Mystic Mandalas you've brought to life with your colours symbolize your personal growth, reflect your emotions, and mark your journey toward mindfulness and inner peace. You have created beautiful art and cultivated a space for relaxation, healing, and self-discovery.

Carry the lessons and tranquillity you've found in these pages into your daily life. Let the calmness and focus you've nurtured here be a source of strength and inspiration. You can return to these pages again or move forward to new creative endeavours. The peace and creativity you've embraced here will always be a part of you.

10 Steps to Colouring
With Conscious Intention

10 Steps to Colouring With Conscious Intention

Welcome to a world of mindful artistry in this Mystic Mandala Adult Colouring Journal, where each page invites you to explore and express yourself creatively and consciously. This unique journal contains 50 simple and more complex Mystic Mandalas, including 17 full-page designs for when you're in the mood for a larger canvas. There are 31 inspiring quotes from artists, spiritual leaders and famous people, 12 thought-provoking writing prompts, and seven affirmations, each crafted to guide you toward a more mindful colouring experience.

As a practice of active meditation, colouring is more than a pastime; it is an act of conscious intention. Whether you're seeking a solo retreat or a shared experience, these pages offer a space to calm your mind and focus your thoughts. It's an opportunity to pause, reflect, and meaningfully engage with your inner self.

As you select your colouring tools – from the gentle shades of coloured pencils to the fluid grace of watercolour pens, the glossy finesse of gel pens, or the nostalgic charm of waxed crayons – remember, each choice is a step in your journey of mindful creation. Feel free to explore the variety available in art stores, online, or specialty shops. Use the blank pages at the end of this journal to experiment with different mediums, observing how each one resonates with your current state of mind. If you're using markers or water-based tools, placing a piece of card stock underneath your work will keep your creations pristine.

The ten transformative steps below outline your guide to colouring with purpose and awareness. They are instructions and pathways to enriching your artistic journey with intention and depth. Every stroke, every choice of colour, is an expression of your present moment, your feelings, and your inner world.

Each Mystic Mandala is a new canvas for your mindful exploration. You may find yourself drawn to colour one mandala meticulously or flow through several in one sitting. It's perfectly fine to start a design, step away to gather your thoughts, and return later with a new perspective. This process is about honouring your pace and being fully present in each moment of creation.

As you embark on this colouring adventure, remember it is a unique journey of self-discovery and expression. Each Mystic Mandala you bring to life is a testament to your conscious engagement with the world around you and within you. And each Mystic Mandala you colour reflects your own unique inner beauty.

So collect your colouring tools, find a cozy spot, and let the world of Mystic Mandalas welcome you into a realm of peace, joy, and boundless creativity. Embrace the tranquillity, joy, and introspection that this mindful journey offers.

1. Take Some Quiet Time.

As you embark on your colouring journey, it's essential to carve out a dedicated quiet time, a special slot in your day where you can engage in your creative process undisturbed. Start by scheduling this time, ensuring that you won't be interrupted. If you share your living space, gently request some privacy by closing the door to your space and asking not to be disturbed.

Choose a space that feels like a personal sanctuary, like a snug corner of your room with plush cushions for added comfort, a serene garden bench surrounded by nature's sounds, or any other place where you feel most at peace. Comfort is key. So settle into a position that supports your posture, perhaps with a supportive chair or a soft cushion that cradles your back.

The time you take is a precious gift to yourself, so eliminate distractions by turning off electronic devices like your phone or TV, allowing you to fully immerse yourself in the calming experience of colouring without any external disturbances. This setup paves the way for a mindful and uninterrupted creative session, where you can genuinely connect with your inner artist and the emotions you wish to express through your art.

2. Prepare Your Space.

To create an ideal setting for your colouring session, focus on enhancing your comfort and ensuring all the necessary items are within reach.

- Begin by preparing your favourite beverage, be it a warm, aromatic cup of tea or a refreshing drink to set the tone for a relaxed experience.
- Play in the background, music you love, selecting tunes that uplift or calm you, depending on your mood.
- Settle into a space where you feel safe and at ease, perhaps surrounded by cushions or sitting in a favourite chair.
- Gather your colouring materials. These might include an array of coloured pencils, markers, or crayons,.
- Organize these tools neatly on your table or in your chosen workspace, ensuring they are easily accessible.
- Enhance the ambiance by lighting a scented candle or prepare a diffuser with your favourite essential oils.

Scent can be crucial in creating a calming atmosphere, and adding gentle background music enhances this effect. Now you have created a setting that is ideal for immersing yourself in the peaceful pleasure of colouring with a mindful purpose.

3. Identify Your Feelings.

Connect with your inner self and emotions to prepare for a reflective experience.

- Close your eyes and take several deep, grounding breaths to be fully present.
- Reflect on your current mental and emotional state, and recognize and accept your feelings without self-criticism.
- Allow your emotions to flow through you, feel them in your in-breath, and release them with your out-breath.
- Engage in honest self-reflection to identify what you need to let go of or welcome into your life (e.g., experiences, relationships, events, states of being).
- Place your hand over your heart, feel its rhythm, and focus your breathing through your heart.
- Breathe slowly and deeply, creating a calm, accepting space within yourself.
- In this tranquil state, let go of what no longer serves you or open your heart to attract what you need or desire.

Use this process as a mental and emotional preparation for the creative and meditative act of colouring, aligning your artistic expression with your innermost thoughts and feelings.

4. Choose Your Quote, Writing Prompt or Affirmation.

Next, take a moment to review the various quotes, writing prompts, or affirmations, looking for that one piece of writing that resonates deeply with your current emotional state. Flip through the pages leisurely, allowing your intuition to guide you. Your chosen words will hold significant meaning for you now, serving as a beacon throughout your creative process. Whether it's an affirmation that lifts your spirits, a thought-provoking quote that challenges your perspectives, or a writing prompt that sparks your imagination, choose the one that aligns most closely with your current feelings and thoughts. This selected writing becomes more than words; it transforms into a guiding light, helping to focus and direct your thoughts and intentions as you colour. It's a tool for introspection and inspiration, echoing your inner voice and enhancing the depth and intentionality of your colouring experience.

5. Let the Colours Pick You.

As you observe the array of colouring tools – pencils, pens, or markers – take a moment to decide which type resonates with your current mood and intention. This choice sets the tone for your creative session. As you gaze upon various colours, let your intuition guide you. Notice which hues capture your attention or evoke a certain feeling within you, regardless of whether they are familiar choices or unexplored territories in your colour palette. Allow yourself to be drawn to attractive colours, even if they differ vastly from your usual selections. Embrace the spontaneity of this moment and trust in your instinctual picks. The key is not to dwell too much on the decision-making process. By choosing the first colour that seems to call out to you, you're engaging with the flow of the moment. Understand that this process has no right or wrong; it's all about what feels suitable for you. The colours you select are not just mere shades; they are reflections of your current state of mind and heart, and they will invariably be the perfect choices for your Mystic Mystic Mandala at this particular moment. This approach encourages a harmonious blend of conscious intention and subconscious expression, making your colouring experience both meaningful and liberating.

6. Colour Your Mystic Mystic Mandala.

As you begin to colour your Mystic Mandala on the opposite page of your chosen quote, writing prompt, or affirmation, prepare to infuse it with the colours you've intuitively selected. Embark on the journey of filling in the unique design of the Mystic Mandala with a mindful approach. As you colour, let each stroke reflect your intention while keeping what your selected quote, prompt, or affirmation means to you. This process is more than rushing to complete the picture or achieving perfection. Instead, it is about immersing yourself in the colouring process. Appreciate how each colour you've chosen interacts with others on the page, and observe the emotions and sensations that arise as you apply them. Lose yourself as you fill out the details of the Mystic Mandala. Experience the therapeutic and meditative effects. Paying attention to how the colours blend, what patterns emerge, and how the overall design evolves with each addition of colour. This approach to colouring your Mystic Mystic Mandala becomes a creative, active meditation, a conduit for inner exploration and expression.

7. Notice Your Process.

As you proceed, take a moment to become deeply aware of your creative process. Observe the starting point of your journey - do you naturally begin at the Mystic Mandala's top, bottom, left, or right? Notice the direction in which your colouring unfolds: do you move from the edge to the center, from the center outwards, or do you follow a specific path clockwise, counterclockwise, or perhaps you take a more random approach? Whether deliberate or instinctual, each choice carries its meaning and reflects a part of your inner self. At the same time, be mindful of the thoughts and emotions that may surface during this creative process. Are you rushing to complete the design, or do you struggle with frustration if the outcome doesn't match your idea of 'perfection'? It's important to acknowledge these feelings and tendencies. Gently remind yourself that colouring with conscious intention transcends the pursuit of perfection; it's about embracing the journey of creation, the joy it brings, and the personal insights it offers. This mindfulness in your approach enhances your colouring experience and allows for a deeper connection with your creative self, making filling in the Mystic Mystic Mandala a reflective and enjoyable journey.

8. Immerse Yourself in the flow.

As you continue to colour your Mystic Mystic Mandala, embrace a state of open receptivity, allowing your thoughts, feelings, and any sudden realizations to

effortlessly emerge, express themselves and flow out of you. Let the chosen colours guide the journey; trust them to lead you intuitively through the sacred pathways of your Mystic Mandala. Allow the next steps in your creative exploration to reveal themselves to you. Simultaneously, immerse yourself entirely in the process of colouring. Pay close attention to any sensory experiences - the texture of the paper beneath your fingers, the harmonious way the colours blend on the page, and the rhythmic, almost dance-like movements of your hand as you apply colour. This activity transcends mere artistic expression; it is part of a meditative practice. Allow yourself to become fully absorbed in the present moment, experiencing a deep sense of presence and mindfulness. This immersion enhances the beauty of your creation. It provides a serene and reflective space where colouring becomes a conduit for your path to inner peace and self-discovery.

9. Complete Your Mystic Mystic Mandala.

Once you reach the point where your Mystic Mystic Mandala feels complete, take a moment to reflect. Did you fill in every space? or leave some empty? Take a step back to absorb and truly appreciate this significant moment. Allow yourself a few deep, grounding breaths to fully embrace your accomplishment. Look at the Mystic Mandala you've created, not just as a piece of art but as a reflection of your inner journey and state of mind at this time. Understand that completion here is subjective and deeply personal. It is not about covering every inch of the design but about feeling that you have adequately experienced your thoughts, emotions, and intentions through this creative process. Your Mystic Mandala's colours, patterns, and overall aesthetic are unique to you and your experience, making it a perfect representation of your inner self. This phase of appreciation and reflection is crucial, as it allows you to recognize and celebrate the beauty and depth of what you have created and the peaceful introspection it has brought into your life today.

10. Celebrate Your Accomplishment!

Upon completing your Mystic Mystic Mandala, whether you consciously perceive a shift within yourself or not, recognize that you have granted your unconscious pure expression through this colouring process. Bringing colour to your Mystic Mandala is more than just an artistic endeavour; it is a more profound, perhaps unspoken, part of your being. Take a moment to celebrate this personal experience, the unique self-expression you've allowed to flow through you. After finishing, step back to appreciate and contemplate your artwork fully. Acknowledge the dedication, time, and range of emotions woven into your Mystic Mandala's fabric. Feel a sense of pride and accomplishment in what you have achieved and your mindful journey in creating this piece. It is a tangible representation of your inner journey, rich with personal meaning and insight. Consider finding a special place to display your Mystic Mandala, where you can see it regularly. Let it stand as a beautiful visual reminder of the tranquillity, creativity, and self-discovery you experienced during this process. It can physically represent your inner growth and colouring with the conscious intention you used. Now infused with your personal touch and emotions, this Mystic Mandala can become a cherished artifact of your journey toward mindfulness and self-expression.

In reflecting upon this journey of colouring your Mystic Mystic Mandala, remember that the true essence of this activity lies in the enjoyment and tranquillity it offers. Each step is an integral part of a more extensive journey. This journey leads you towards greater mindfulness and self-expression. It allows you to explore the depths of your emotions and thoughts, express them in a tangible form, and find peace and contentment. As you engage in this practice, let yourself absorb the serene joy it brings. Allow each colouring session to be a personal retreat, a momentary pause from the hustle of everyday life where you can reconnect with yourself. Colouring becomes a creative, meditative, and reflective practice, offering tranquillity and self-discovery. So, as you pick up your colouring tools, do so with a light heart and an open mind. Embrace the peace, joy, and myriad of colours this journey brings. Happy colouring, and may you find bliss in every stroke and hue that flows from your heart to your Mystic Mandala.

31 Mystic Mandalas
for Pure Prosperity
Inspirational Quotes

Pure Prosperity Inspirational Quotes

5 Steps to Working with Inspirational Quotes

Inspirational quotes are like little drops of wisdom that can positively impact your thoughts and feelings anytime and anywhere. They are powerful because they can connect with your current feelings or circumstances. Think of these famous thinkers, celebrities, or spiritual leaders who have uttered these words as helpful advisors. Their words can illuminate different viewpoints and ideas, uplift your spirit, and lend a new perspective as they share your experiences.

In this Adult Colouring Journal, you'll find 31 inspirational quotes paired with a Mystic Mandala to colour to boost your creative process.

Reading a good quote can offer another perspective on a tricky situation or a challenging experience. Inspirational quotes can even nudge you to think or act differently, especially when stuck on something. For instance, an inspirational quote might encourage you to be kinder to yourself or see a problem in a different light. This new understanding can bring you a sense of calm and clarity.

The more you focus on an inspirational quote, the more it can inspire and motivate you. Over time, inspirational quotes can increase your awareness of essential truths and insights.

If you want to get the most out of these quotes, here is a simple five-step plan for you to follow:

1. Choose:

Select a quote that speaks to you and relates to your current circumstances or situation.

2. Practice

Read the quote aloud or repeat it in your head three to five times. Accentuate different words each time to shift their meaning.

3. Reflect

Break down the words in the inspirational quote and consider what each one means to you personally.

4. Refer

Refer to the inspirational quote throughout your colouring practice for a little boost.

5. Apply

Relate the quote's meaning to your daily life. Consider how its message can help your everyday activities beyond your present colouring practice.

Incorporating inspirational quotes into your daily life can be a powerful yet subtle tool for self-awareness. These words of wisdom can guide you, lift your spirits, and even help you make positive changes in your life. Each inspirational quote is a beacon of wisdom and encouragement, guiding you through your colouring session and beyond.

Using inspirational quotes while colouring your Mystic Mandalas is a fun and creative activity and a simple tool for personal growth and mindfulness. Following the steps outlined above, you can transform your colouring experience into a meaningful journey of self-discovery and reflection.

Colouring the Mystic Mandalas offers a meditative escape, allowing you to express your emotions creatively about each quote. Remember, this process is about more than just creating art; it's about nurturing your soul, enhancing your well-being, and embracing the joy of living in the moment.

So select your colours, choose your quotes, and embark on this delightful journey of colour and words. Let each Mystic Mandala and inspirational quote uplift you, guide you, and inspire a brighter, more mindful path forward.

"

If you want greater
prosperity in your life,
start forming a vacuum
to receive it.

~Catherine Ponder~

99

Equality and prosperity
shouldn't be seen as
enemies of each other,
but as partners.
One reinforces the other.

~Anonymous~

99

There are many roads
to prosperity,
but one must be taken.
Inaction leads nowhere.

~Robert Zoellick~

99

Innovation makes the world go round. It brings prosperity and freedom.

~Robert Metcalf~

99

Prosperity is not without
many fears and distates;
adversity not without many
comforts and hopes.

~Francis Bacon~

"

Prosperity is the measure
or touchstone of virtue,
for it is less difficult to
bear misfortune than to
remain uncorrupted
by pleasure.

~Tacitus~

99

"I am thankful every moment
as much as we need a
prosperous economy,
we also need a prosperity
of kindness and decency."

~Caroline Kernnedy~

99

The key to abundance is
meeting limited circumstances
with unlimited thoughts.

~Marianne Williamson~

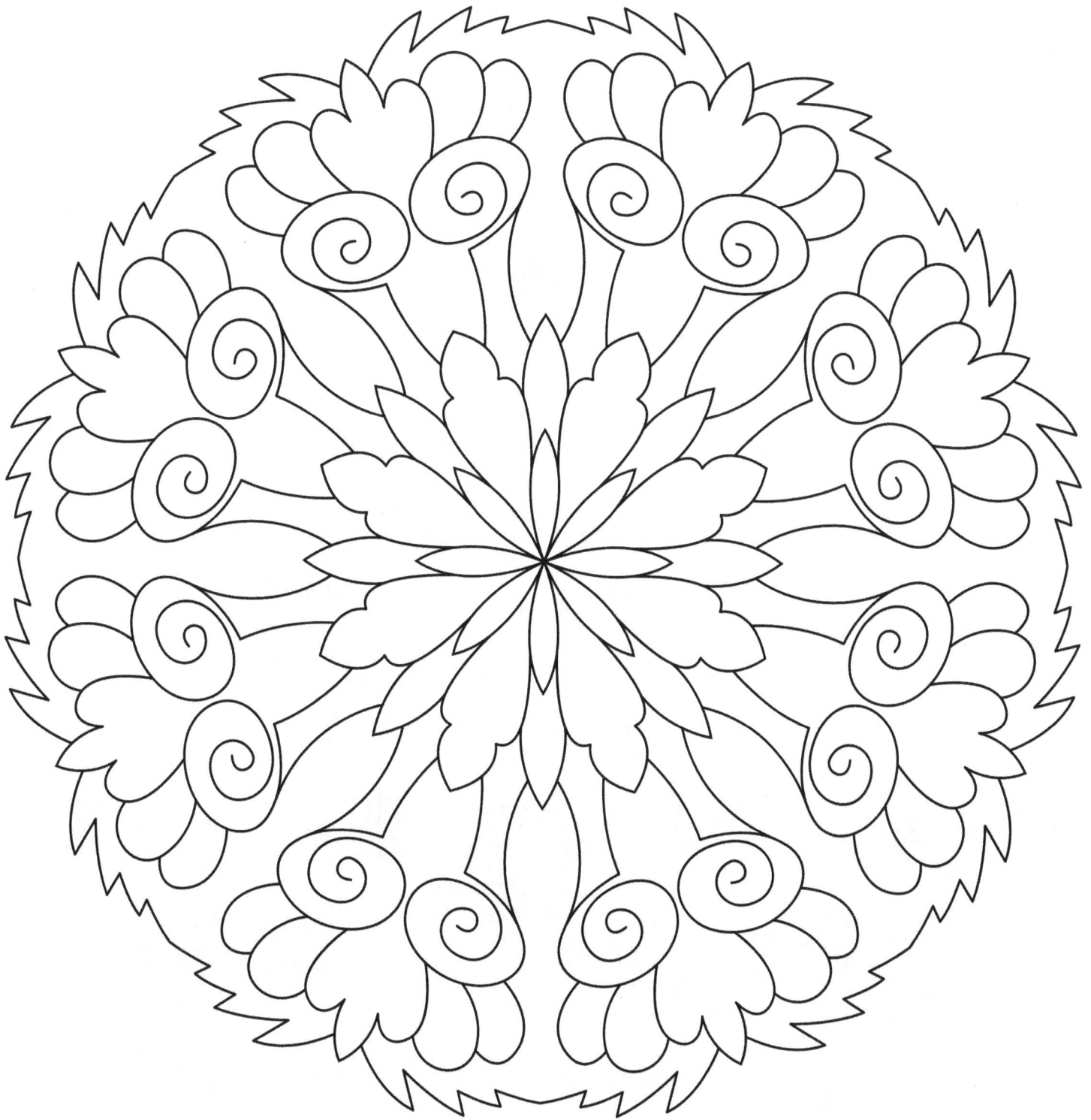

99

The test of our progress
is not whether we add
more to the abundance of
those who have much,
it is whether we provide
enough for those
who have little.

~Franklin D. Roosevelt~

99

Abundance is a process
of letting go;
that which is empty
can receive.

~Bryant H. McGill~

99

~Elevating the status of
women is our best
path to peace, justice,
and prosperity
on a global scale.

~David Horsey~

99

Wealth is the ability to fully experience life.

~Henry David Thoreau~

99

Talent is always conscious
of its own abundance,
and does not object
to sharing.

~Aleksandre Sozhenitsyn~

"

From abundance springs
satiety.

~Livy~

99

Not what we have but
what we enjoy, constitutes
our abundance.

~Epicurus~

99

Not what we have but
what we enjoy, constitutes
our abundance.

~Epicurus~

99

Expect your every need
to be met.
Expect the answer to
every problem,
expect abundance
on every level.

~Eileen Caddy~

99

To live a pure unselfish life, one must count nothing as one's own in the midst of abundance.

~Buddha~

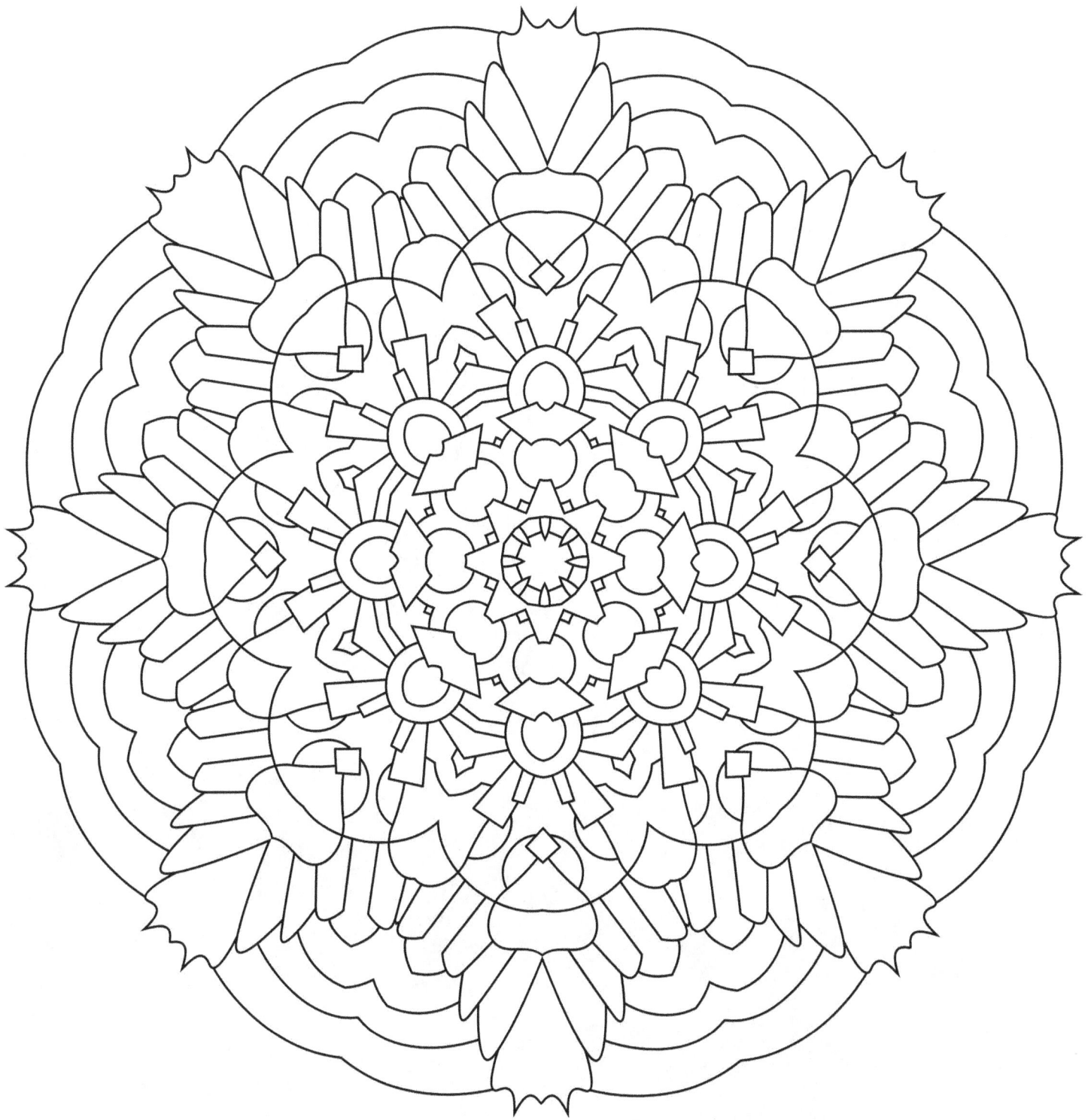

99

Life in abundance comes
only through great love.

~Elbert Hubbard~

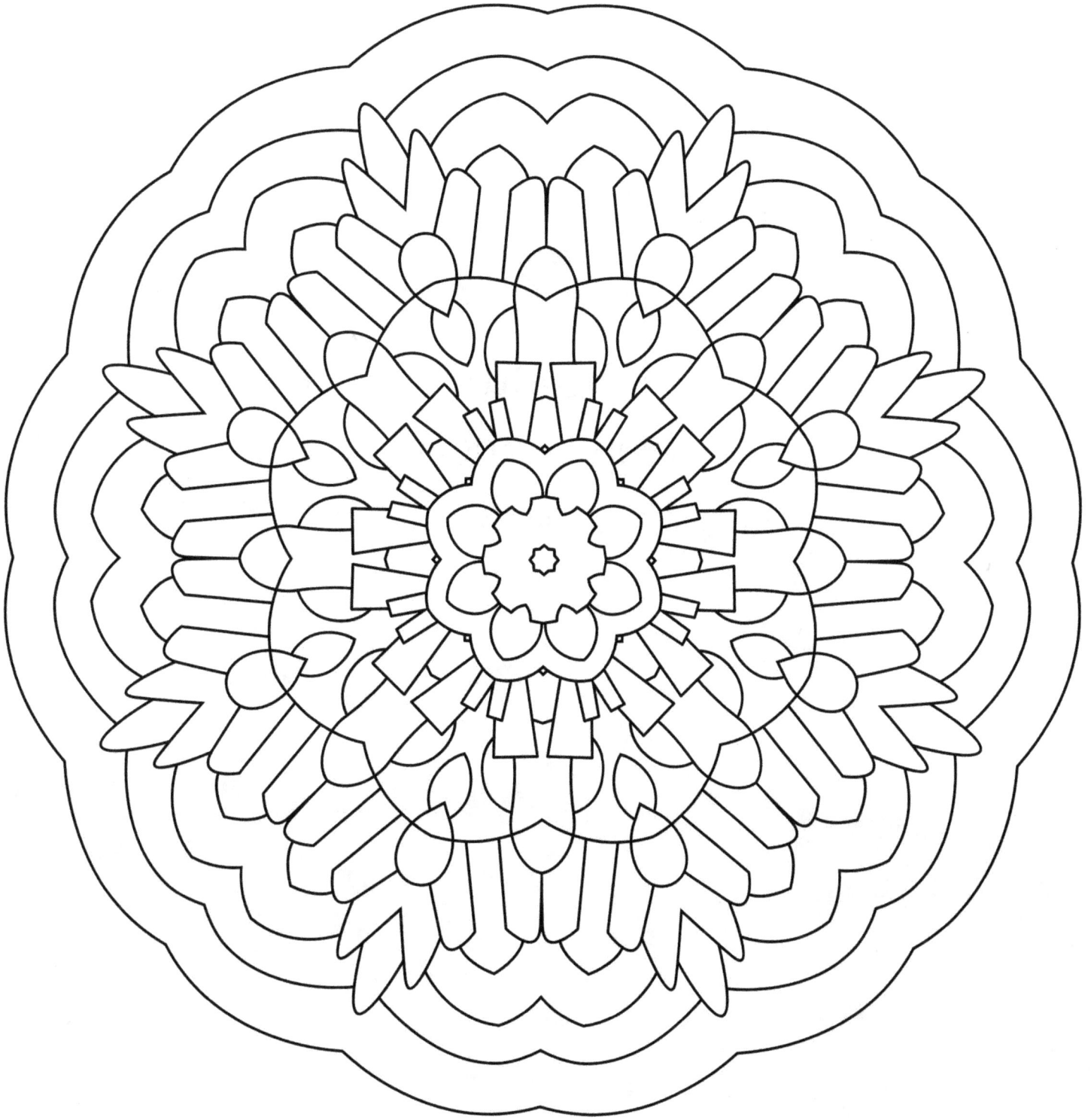

99

Wine is connected to abundance.

~Carole Bouquet~

99

I always was a rich person because money's not related to happiness.

~Paulo Coelho~

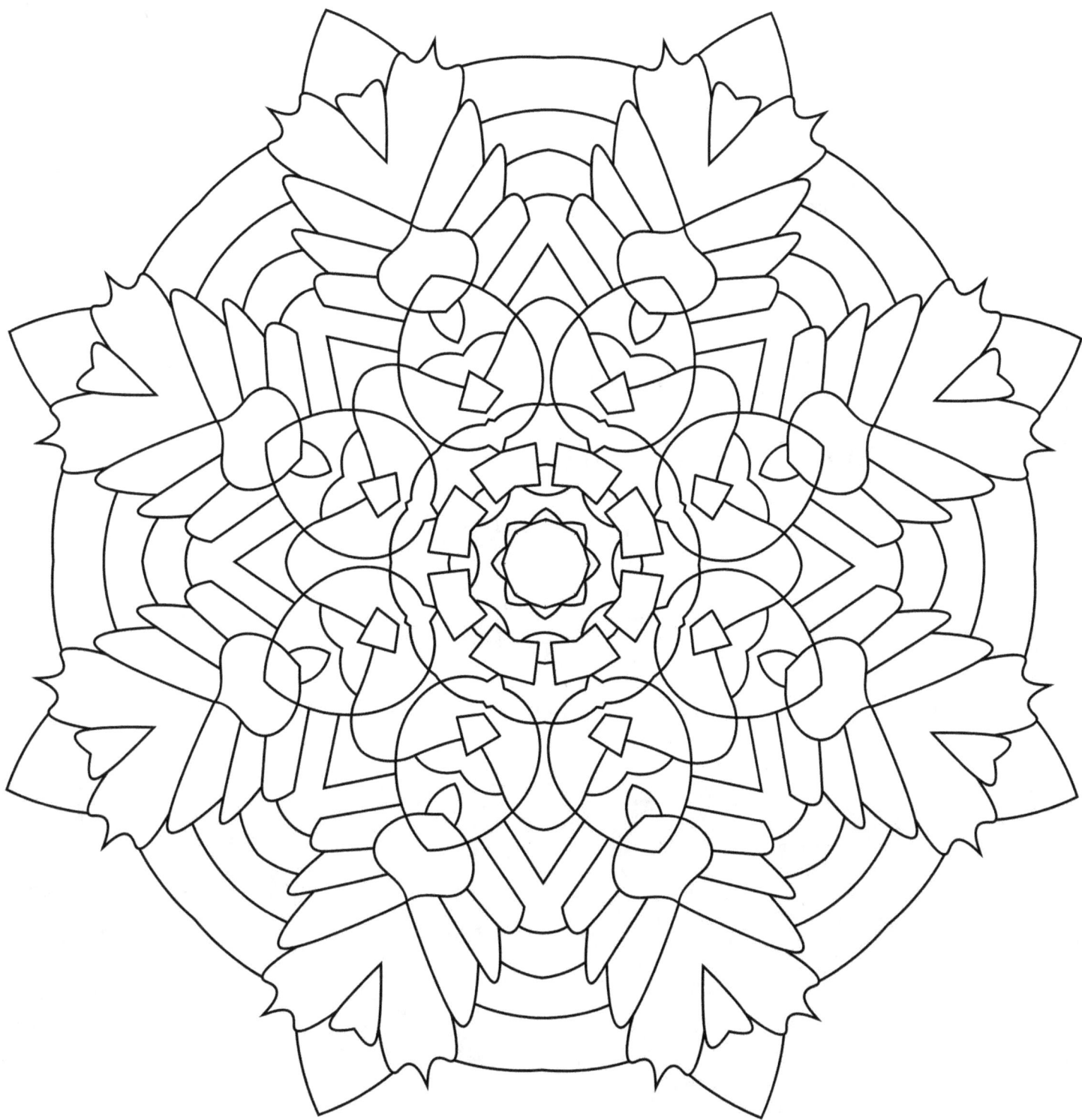

99

You CAN have it all.
You just can't have it all
at once.

~Oprah Winfrey~

99

Adversity has the effect of
eliciting talents,
which in prosperous
circumstances would have
lain dormant.

~Horace~

99

When I chased after money,
I never had enough.
When I got my life on
purpose and focused on giving
of myself and everything that
arrived into my life,
then I was prosperous.

~Wayne Dyer~

99

It is not the ship so
much as the skillful sailing
that assures
the prosperous voyage.

~George William Curtis~

"

Doing what you love is
the cornerstone of
abundance in your life.

~Wayne Dyer~

"

In order to become
prosperous, a person must
initially work very hard, so
he or she has to sacrifice
a lot of leisure time.

~Dalai Lama~

99

An idealist is a person who helps other people to be prosperous."

~Henry Ford~

99

If the human race wishes
to have a prolonged and
indefinite period of material
prosperity, they have only
got to behave in a
peaceful and, helpful way
toward one another.

~Winston Churchill~

99

Opportunity today, prosperity tomorrow.

~Julian Castro~

99

Globalism began as a vision
of a world with free trade,
shared prosperity,
and open borders.
These are good, even
noble things to aim for.

~Deepak Chopra~

12 Mystic Mandalas
for Pure Prosperity
Writing Prompts

Pure Prosperity Writing Prompts

5 Steps to Working with Writing Prompts

Writing with prompts can be a beneficial and powerful way to understand yourself better. Writing prompts help you to focus on something specific. When you use writing prompts to think about a current or past situation, you can discover new things about yourself.

Writing prompts can help you write down your thoughts clearly and concisely. You can remember things more deeply and see them differently as you write. This new way of looking at your experiences can make you feel stronger and help you heal in a gentle and supportive way.

Sometimes, it can be hard to face some experiences directly. Writing prompts can make it easier, and this practice can lead to increased self-awareness, healing, and closure.

If you would like to write with a deeper purpose, here are five simple steps to help you get more out of the experience:

1. Prepare

Choose a time for your writing practice when you won't be disturbed. The time could be early in the morning before your activities begin or end your day. Choose a space where you feel relaxed and comfortable. It could be a cozy corner of your room, a spot by a window, or even outdoors in nature. Make your space inviting and conducive to reflection – maybe light a candle, have a warm cup of tea ready, or have some gentle music playing in the background.

2. Choose

Let the theme of this Mystic Mandala Adult Colouring Journal guide your writing. Before you start, browse the journal and pick a prompt that resonates with you. Think about what you want to achieve with your writing – are you

seeking clarity, healing, or inspiration? Your intention will help guide your choice of prompt. For example, choose a prompt encouraging action or change if you seek motivation.

3. Embrace

Approach your writing with an open mind, free from expectations about a particular outcome. Write at a pace that feels natural to you. There's no need to rush or fill the whole page. Focus on being honest and authentic in your expression. Resist the temptation to edit yourself as you write; just let your thoughts and feelings flow onto the paper. Remember, this is your personal space for expression, so there's no right or wrong way to do it.

4. Express

Write as if you're talking to yourself without holding back. Writing gives you a chance to be completely honest. Acknowledge that truth can be challenging to express, but it's also where healing and understanding start. If you feel resistant, take a short break and focus instead on colouring the Mystic Mandala on the opposite page. When you feel ready again, gently return to your writing. This place is a safe space to explore your deepest thoughts and feelings.

5. Integrate

Pay attention to the emotions and thoughts as you colour your Mystic Mandala. Decide whether you want to write before you start colouring, during the process, or after you've completed your Mystic Mandala. Each method offers a different perspective that can enrich your experience. For example, writing beforehand can set the tone for your colouring, while writing afterward can be a reflection on the experience. Trust your intuition to guide you in choosing the right moment. Once you've finished both colouring and writing, spend some time reviewing your work. Look for connections between the colours you selected, the patterns you created, and the words you wrote. This writing can offer you deeper insights into your emotions and thoughts.

By following the steps above, you can deepen your experience with the Mystic Mandala Adult Colouring Journal, turning it into a meaningful practice of self-exploration and mindfulness.

Incorporating writing prompts into your personal growth journey offers a unique and enriching experience beyond mere self-expression. This practice, particularly when combined with the mindful activity of colouring Mystic Mandalas, can become a powerful tool for introspection, healing, and empowerment.

Writing prompts allow you to explore your thoughts and emotions deeply. You can uncover new layers of understanding about yourself and your experiences. This guided writing process can lead to surprising discoveries and help you clarify complex feelings or situations. It is one way to honestly and authentically engage with your inner self in a safe, judgment-free space.

The benefits of this practice extend beyond the moments of writing and colouring. The insights gained can impact your daily life, enhancing self-awareness and fostering a more grounded and centred approach to challenges. As you reflect on the prompts and bring colour to the Mystic Mandalas, you engage in a creative and active meditation that calms your mind and nurtures your soul.

Additionally, this practice can help you de-stress and alleviate anxiety. It offers a constructive outlet for emotions. This practice can help you develop a more vital self-awareness, resilience, and emotional intelligence.

Finally, remember that your journey with writing prompts and Mystic Mandalas is uniquely yours. There's no right or wrong way to approach it, and you can tailor each session to meet your current needs and mood. Whether seeking healing, understanding, or a peaceful escape, this practice can be valuable for personal growth.

So, embrace this opportunity to explore your inner world through the power of words and colours.

Let each prompt guide you to new realizations, and let each Mystic Mandala reflect the beauty and complexity of your innermost thoughts.

What does Pure Prosperity mean to you?

What awareness do you
have of the abundance that
surrounds you?

When did you first attract (earn) money and how did it make you feel?

What I have learned about having financial abundance is ...

What action could you take today to experience more abundance and prosperity?

How was prosperity modelled
to you as a child?

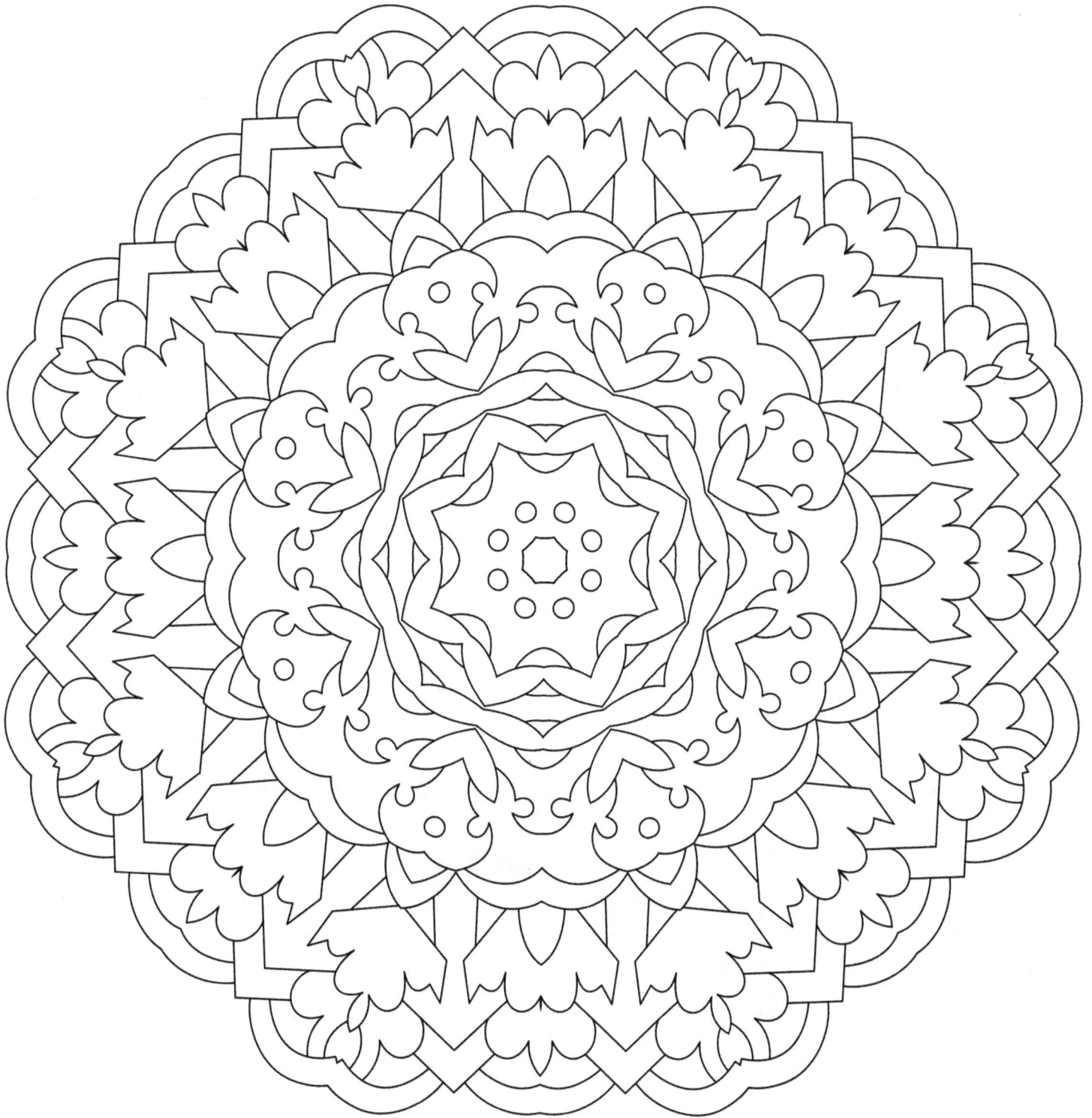

How would the world be different if everyone lived in abundance and prosperity?

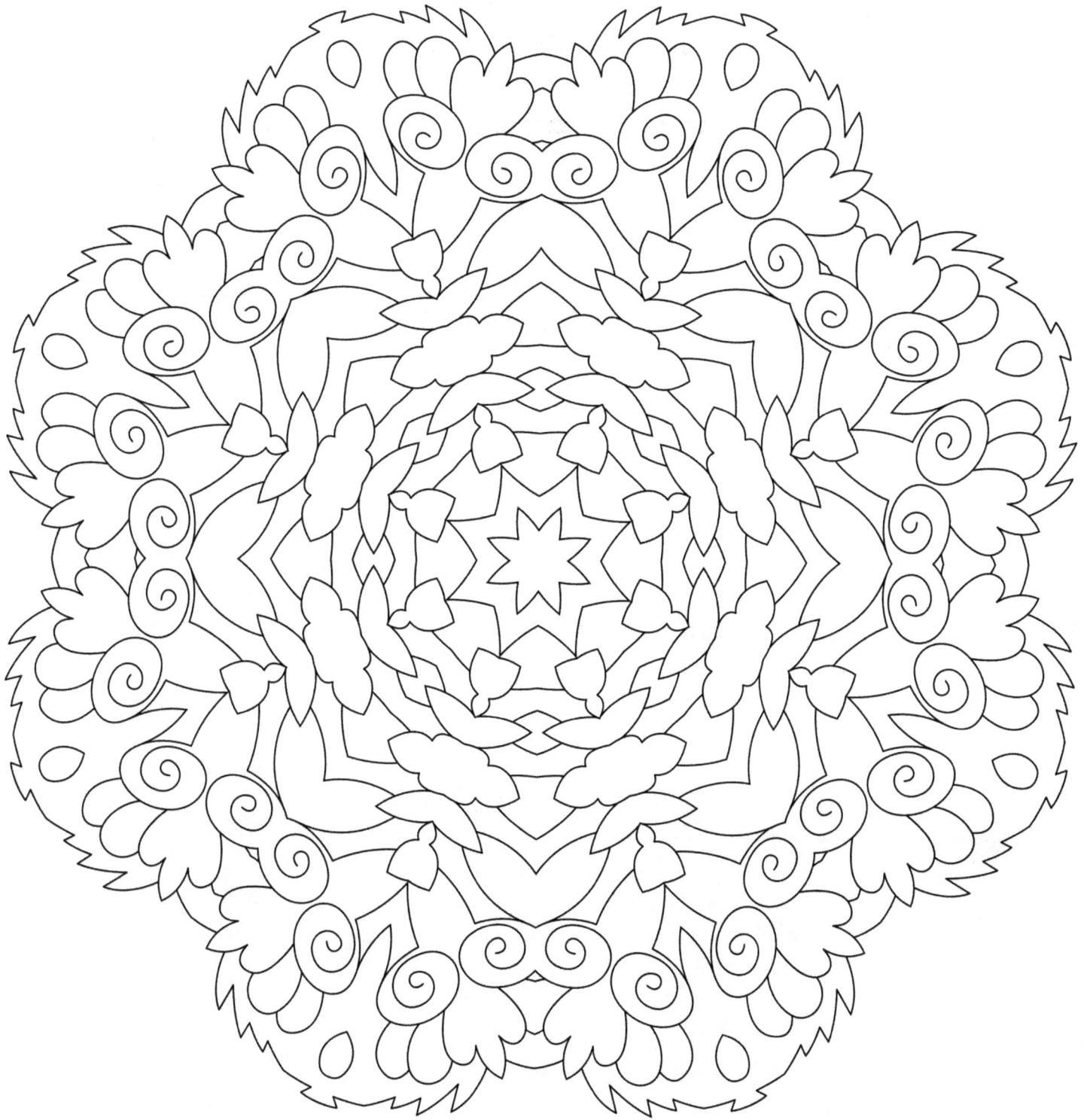

What is your preferred form of Pure Prosperity?

Who do you think is a good
example of a prosperous life,
dead or alive, and why?

What past experience made you feel prosperous and what do you need to repeat it?

What past experience that led to a feeling of prosperity would you like to repeat?

If you had unlimited abundance and prosperity, how would that change your life?

_____
_____
_____
_____
_____
_____
_____
_____
_____
_____
_____
_____
_____
_____
_____
_____
_____
_____
_____
_____
_____
_____
_____
_____
_____

7 Mystic Mandalas
for Pure Prosperity
Affirmations

Pure Prosperity Affirmations

5 Steps to Working With Affirmations

Affirmations are a simple yet powerful tool for personal growth and positive change. In our fast-paced lives, it's easy to get caught up in negative thought patterns that can hold us back. That's where affirmations come in – positive statements, phrases, or sentences you repeat to yourself, designed to overcome negative thoughts and foster a mindset geared towards success and happiness.

You practice affirmations anytime and anywhere. Whether starting your day, taking a break at work, or winding down at night. You can tailor affirmations to focus on your goals, from boosting self-confidence and self-esteem to attracting love, success, and abundance into your life.

Remember that the power of affirmations lies in their consistent practice. Just as negative thoughts can shape our reality over time, so can positive affirmations – in a way that enhances and enriches our lives. By choosing words that resonate with your aspirations and repeating them regularly, you can gradually transform your inner belief system, leading to tangible, positive changes in your life.

Below is a simple yet effective five-step process to make the most out of the affirmations provided in this Mystic Mandala Adult Colouring Journal, ensuring that you harness their full potential for personal growth and positive change.

1 Prepare

Before you start, find a peaceful place to focus without interruptions. Find a quiet room, a cozy corner of your home, or even a peaceful spot outdoors. Adding soft music or lighting ensures your environment is comfortable and inviting. Begin by centring yourself with a breathing exercise: inhale deeply for six counts, hold for a moment, and then exhale slowly for eight counts. This breathing pattern helps to calm your mind and body, creating a receptive state for your affirmations.

2 Select

Choose an affirmation that resonates with your current feelings, challenges, or goals. The affirmation should feel meaningful and relevant to your current situation or circumstances. Take your time to browse through the affirmations and pick one that genuinely speaks to you and aligns with your intentions.

3 Declare

Once you've selected your affirmation, declare it aloud or silently. Saying it out loud can be more impactful as it allows you to hear and internalize the words more fully. Speak with confidence and belief, as if you already embody the affirmation. Certainty helps to reinforce the affirmation's message and embed it in your subconscious mind.

4 Repeat

Repeat your chosen affirmation three to five times, concentrating on each word. As you repeat the words, visualize what they represent. Imagine yourself living and feeling the truth of the affirmation. For instance, if your affirmation concerns peace, picture yourself as calm and serene. This visualization technique, combined with repetition, strengthens the affirmation's effect.

5 Integrate

After repeating your affirmation, close your practice with another round of deep breathing.

- Inhale and exhale slowly
- allowing the essence of the affirmation to integrate into your mind and heart.
- Imagine the words of the affirmation flowing through you with each breath, solidifying their impact.

This step is crucial as it helps seal the practice, ensuring the affirmation resonates within you throughout your day.

Affirmations can be a powerful tool for personal transformation and empowerment, especially when combined with the mindful practice of colouring Mystic Mandalas. By following the five-step process for affirmations and integrating this with colouring the Mystic Mandala on the opposite page, you create a multi-faceted approach to self-discovery and positive change.

The act of colouring, with its meditative and calming effects, complements the affirmations, allowing you to embody their messages fully. As you focus on the colours and patterns, visualize the affirmations taking root in your life, enhancing the transformative power of the words.

This combined practice of affirmations and colouring is a powerful method for reinforcing positive beliefs and intentions. The Mystic Mandalas visually represent the growth and change you cultivate through affirmations. As you colour, imagine the affirmations intertwining with the designs to create a vibrant creation of personal growth and well-being.

Embrace this journey with an open heart and mind, allowing the affirmations and the Mystic Mandalas to guide you toward self-discovery, growth, and fulfillment. This integrated approach promotes a more profound inner peace and opens avenues for creativity, self-expression, and mindfulness.

Revel in your transformational journey, where every affirmation you recite, and every Mandala you colour bring you closer to realizing your true potential and creating the life you envision.

Opportunities for
Prosperity and Abundance
fill my life

I attract abundance from multiple sources in multiple ways

I happily share my prosperity and abundance with those around me

I attract Abundance and Pure Prosperity every day and in every way

I am grateful for all the abundance that surrounds me and mine

My prosperous feelings
attract more prosperity

My life is abundant and prosperous in every way

Thank You

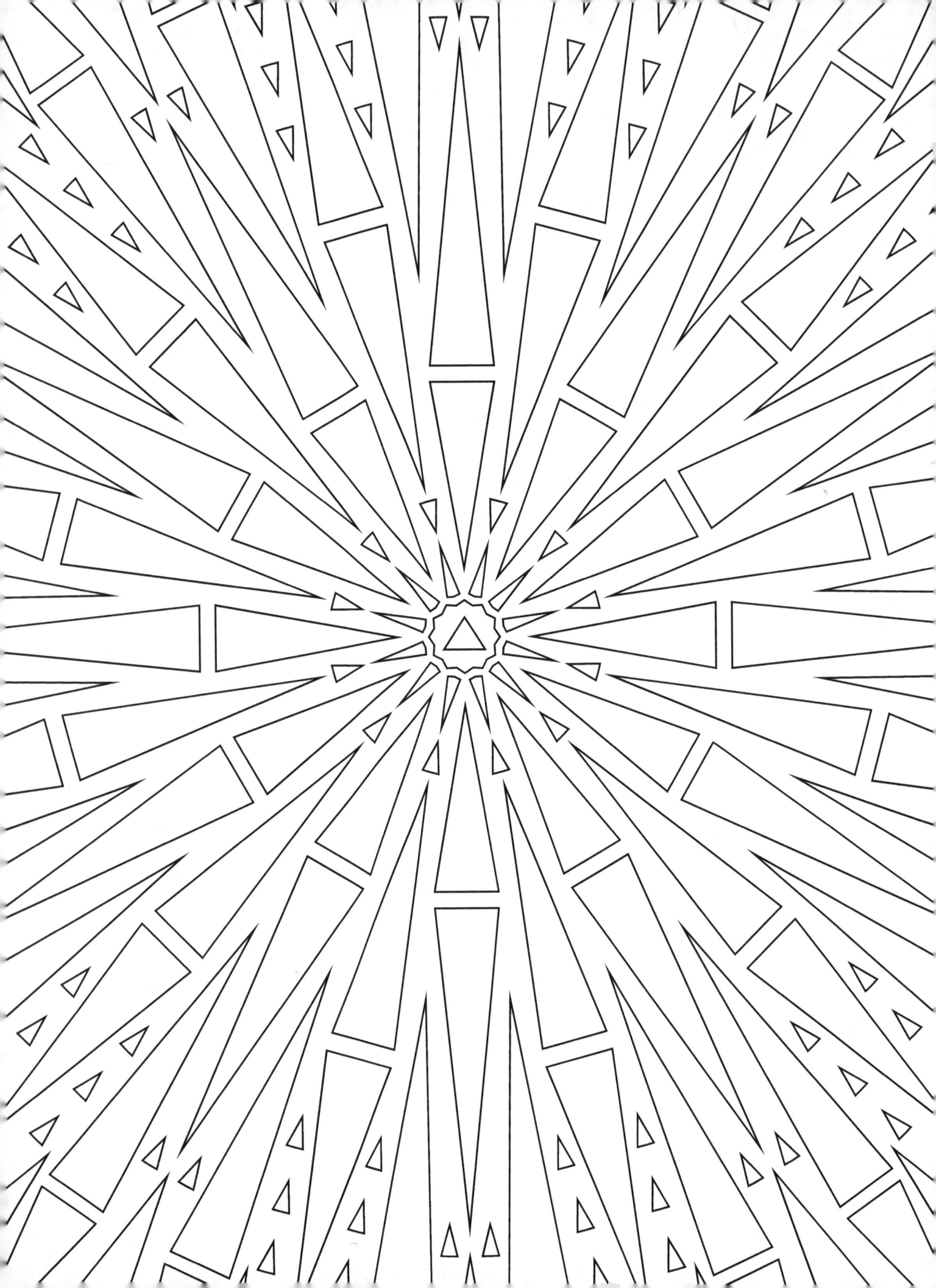

Thank You

Thank you for buying this Mystic Mandalas Adult Colouring Journal.

Please take a moment and leave a review on Amazon, as reviews help independent authors reach more readers.

You are welcome to submit any ideas, comments or suggestions to me at ImagoMysticArts.com.

We are always looking for ways to improve products for our customers.

Feel free to send me any pictures of your finished Mystic Mandalas, with your comments, to ImagoMysticArts.com, as it inspires me to see what beauty you create with your choice of colours for the Mystic Mandalas.

Thank you for allowing me to support you in Creating with Conscious Intention.

Blessings,
Patricia

FOLLOW ME!

Want a FREE Gift?

Unlock the Magic of my Healing Harp Music for **FREE!** Email info@imagomysticarts.com with 'Pure Prosperity' in the subject line of your email, and I will send you an exclusive MP3 album of "**Winter's Bride**," a recording of my original Celtic Harp compositions so that you have healing music to accompany your colouring practice!

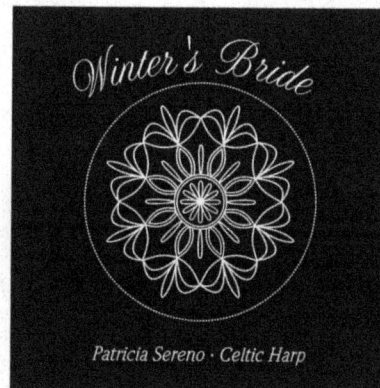

Only available through this FREE offer

About the Author

Patricia Sereno has studied spirituality, esoteric philosophy and Jungian archetypes for over 35 years. With these influences, Patricia has maintained an international practice as a professional astrologer since 1988, specializing in psycho-spiritual astrology. Other published achievements include books for children, poetry and astrology. An accomplished musician with the Celtic harp, Patricia composes healing music and has produced three solo albums.

Patricia lived and travelled abroad for more than a decade, exposing her to various cultures and enriching her life experience. Despite any perceived differences, she also learned about the universal themes that connect all races, cultures, and belief systems.

Patricia's creative works and astrology practice have allowed her to help others navigate life challenges, increase self-awareness, and maximize their potential.

You can contact Patricia directly through her website:

ImagoMysticArts.com.

More Mystic Mandalas

30-Day Journals

30 DAYS OF GENTLE GRIEF

30 DAYS OF GRATITUDE

30 DAYS OF FORGIVENESS

30 DAYS OF PROSPERITY

Adult Colouring Journals

CERTAIN COURAGE

CONSCIOUS CREATIVITY

FIERCE FORGIVENESS

GRACIOUS GRATITUDE

GENTLE GRIEF

KNOWING KINDNESS

LIMITLESS LOVE

PURE PROSPERITY

SIMPLE SERENITY

For the most recent Colouring Journals Please visit ImagoMysticArts.com

Colour Test Page

Colour Test Page